NO LONGER PROPERTY OF

ANYTHINK LIBRARIES /
RANGEVIEW LIBRARY DISTRICT

D0475223

A TIMELINE OF

GUNS, MISSILES, AND ROCKETS

by Tim Cooke

CAPSTONE PRESS

a capstone imprint

Edge Books are published by Capstone Press,
1710 Roe Crest Drive, North Mankato, Minnesota 56003
www.capstonepub.com

Published in 2018 by Capstone Publishing Ltd

Copyright © 2018 Brown Bear Books Ltd

All rights reserved. No part of this book may be reproduced, stored in a retrieval system, or
transmitted in any form or by any means, electronic, mechanical, photocopying, recording, or
otherwise, now or in the future, without the prior written permission of the copyright holder.

Library of Congress Cataloging-in-Publication Data
Cataloging-in-publication information is on file with the Library of Congress.

ISBN: 978-1-5157-9197-3 (library binding)
ISBN: 978-1-5157-9203-1 (eBook PDF)

For Brown Bear Books Ltd:
Managing Editor: Tim Cooke
Designer: John Woolford
Editorial Director: Lindsey Lowe
Design Manager: Keith Davis
Children's Publisher: Anne O'Daly
Picture Manager: Sophie Mortimer
Production Director: Alastair Gourlay

Photo Credits
Front Cover: Department of Defense: cr; Dreamstime: Martin Brayley tc; Shutterstock: Chris Alcock cl, Militarist bc.

Interior: Alamy: SPUTNIK 19cr; Boeing: 26br; Department of Defense: 1, 21tr, 22-23, 22bc, 23tr, 23bl, 24-25, 25tr,
26-27, 27tr, 27br, 29tr, 29br; Dreamstime: Martin Brayley 6-7, Oleg Doroshin/Dovoo 20-21t, Jorg Hackermann/
Meinzahn 16-17; Fabrique Nationale: 28br; Mike Helms: 8br; NASA: 20bc; Raytheon: 25br; Robert Hunt Library: 9tr,
9bc, 10br, 11cr, 12br, 13tr, 14br, 15tr, 16br, 17tr, 17bc, 18bc, 20-21b; Shutterstock: Aleks49 14-15, Chris Alcock
12-13, Art Mari 4, Jeff Gyname 6bc, Pete Hoffman 10-11, Kimchenko Klim 24br, Militarist 18-18, 19br, 28-29, Jon
Nicholls Photography 7tr, Stocksnapper 10bl; Thinkstock: Photos.com 5tr; Thomastock: 7bc, 8-9, 13bc; University
of Oklahoma Library: 5bl.

Brown Bear Books has made every attempt to contact the copyright holders.
If you have any information please contact licensing@brownbearbooks.co.uk

Printed in the USA
5607/AG/17

TABLE OF CONTENTS

EARLY DEVELOPMENT

The first weapons used against targets farther away than an arm's length were stones and spears. They were thrown at animals for hunting and at enemy warriors during warfare. Early peoples developed ways to throw **missiles** farther. They included bows and arrows.

In 1161 the Chinese first used gunpowder. Gunpowder was made of the powdered chemicals saltpeter, charcoal, and sulfur. When the powder particles mixed with oxygen in the air, it created an explosion. In the barrel of a gun, this explosive energy propelled a bullet at high speed out of the end of the barrel toward a target. This principle is the basis of modern guns, missiles, and rockets.

GUNPOWDER WEAPONS

The first Chinese gunpowder weapons were rockets. They resembled modern fireworks. They were not very accurate, and they were mainly used to scare the enemy by making loud noises. By the late 1100s, the rockets had become more accurate. Armies in China and India were using gunpowder weapons to kill their enemies.

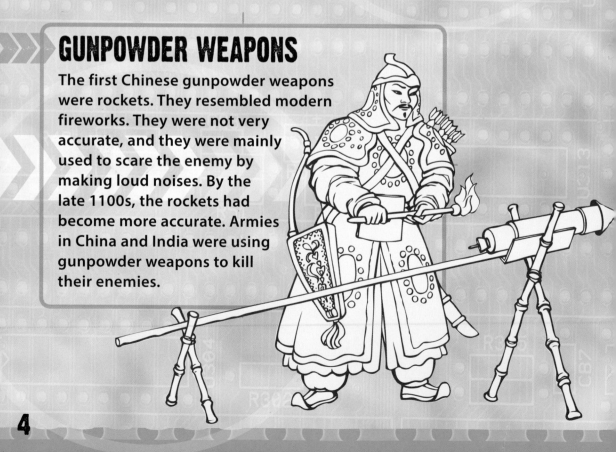

THE FIRST ARTILLERY

Gunpowder was introduced to Europe in the 1200s by Mongols from central Asia. European scientists soon came up with new mixtures of gunpowder. This gunpowder created a bigger explosion than Chinese gunpowder. Europeans used it to fire cannonballs from cannons. The English used the first cannons in the Battle of Crécy against the French in 1346.

HAND GUNS

At the end of the 1400s, soldiers began to carry personal firearms. These hand cannons were heavy and inaccurate. When they were fired, they were so hot they could not be used again until they cooled down.

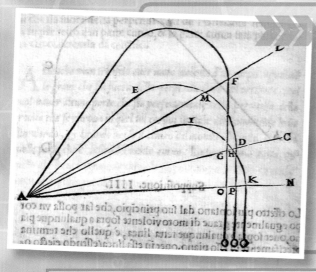

SCIENCE OF GUNS

In the 1600s Italian scientist Galileo Galilei figured out the path a cannonball might take through the air (left). This began the science of ballistics. Ballistics is the study of how missiles such as bullets fly. The science helped the military to develop more accurate weapons.

missile—an object that is thrown or fired toward a target

FIRST FIREARMS

By the mid-1500s, European gunmakers were making both long-barreled guns called muskets and short-barreled pistols. They were fired by lighting a small charge of gunpowder.

In 1610 the first true flintlock was developed. When the user pulled the trigger of the flintlock, a vertical hammer holding a flint, or stone, fell forward into the firing pan at the back of the gun. The hammer created a spark, which set fire to a gunpowder charge inside the barrel. The explosion forced a metal ball, called shot, out of the barrel at high speed. Early flintlock weapons were not very accurate.

HAMMER containing hard flint strikes the firing pan, creating a spark.

PISTOL uses the same flintlock mechanism as the musket.

TIMELINE

1400s
MATCHLOCK GUN
The matchlock gun is developed. It is fired by lighting gunpowder in a firing pan using a burning match, or wick.

1540
FIRST RIFLING
Rifled weapons are invented to try to make a more accurate weapon for hunting.

1808 PAGET CAVALRY FLINTLOCK
Weight: 5 pounds (2.28 kilograms)
Length: 33.75 inches
(85.7 centimeters)
Caliber: 0.660 inches
Loading: Muzzle loading

INSIDE OUT

METAL RAMROD is used to push gunpowder and shot into position down the gun barrel.

BATTLE FORMATION

Early handguns were inaccurate. Armies made up for this by having many soldiers fire at the same time. Soldiers learned to arrange themselves in long lines on the battlefield. When they received the order, they all fired a **volley** at the same time. There was more chance of at least some bullets hitting the target.

1610 ▶▶▶

FLINTLOCK

The flintlock appears. A mechanism creates a spark that propels a bullet down the barrel.

1776 ▶▶▶

U.S. REVOLUTION

American soldiers fight the British Army using mainly flintlock muskets and pistols.

rifled—with a spiral groove carved inside the barrel
volley—a number of bullets or other missiles all fired at the same time

RIFLES

As early as 1540, gunmakers had found that spinning a bullet would make it fly straighter through the air. In the mid-1800s this technology was common in long-barreled guns.

In the 1500s gunmakers carved spirals inside the barrel of the gun to cause the bullet to spin through the air when fired. However, the results were still not very accurate. In the 1840s the Minié ball was invented. Despite its name, the ball was long and cone-shaped, rather than round. The ball fit snugly into the barrel, which made the rifling more effective. By the 1840s and 1850s, old **smoothbore** muskets had their barrels rifled. By the 1860s, rifles were in common use.

BARREL has sockets ready to be fitted with a sword **bayonet** for fighting at close quarters.

LEVER behind the trigger is lowered to load the gun, then raised to make it ready to fire.

TIMELINE

1825

PERCUSSION CAPS
Guns become more reliable with the use of percussion caps. These small explosive charges are detonated by a sharp point when the trigger is pulled, firing a bullet.

1857

FIRST U.S. CARTRIDGE
The first cartridges are produced in the United States. They combine an explosive charge and a bullet in a single piece of ammunition.

SPECIFICATIONS

MARTINI-HENRY

Weight: 8 pounds 7 ounces
  (3.83 kilograms)
Length: 49 inches
  (124.5 centimeters)
Action: Single-shot, breech-loading
Rate of fire: 12 rounds per minute
Effective range: 400 yards
  (370 meters)
Caliber: 0.45 inches

INSIDE OUT

RIFLED BARRELS

Spiral grooves carved into the inside of a gun barrel cause a bullet to spin in the air. Bullets from smoothbore weapons tumble over themselves as they fly and do not follow a straight course. A spinning rifle bullet flies straighter, making rifles far more accurate than earlier weapons.

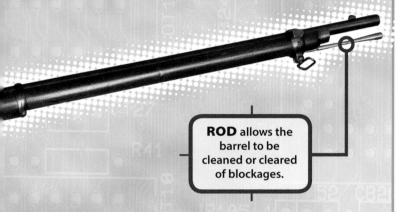

ROD allows the barrel to be cleaned or cleared of blockages.

1860 »»

REPEATING RIFLE

The Spencer Carbine repeating rifle is produced in the United States. Its seven bullets are moved into position by raising a lever.

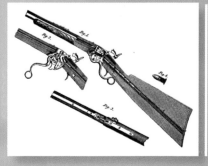

1861 »»

U.S. CIVIL WAR

The main small arms used in the American Civil War (1861–1865) are rifles and hand guns called revolvers.

smoothbore—having no rifling inside the barrel
bayonet—a long, sharp blade attached to the front of a rifle for stabbing

REVOLVERS

Short-barreled handguns were easier to carry and use than long-barreled rifles. However, all muzzle-loading guns still took time to load. This problem was solved in 1836, when Samuel Colt invented the revolver.

The first revolver could store up to six bullets in a **cylinder** linked to the trigger and firing mechanism. The cylinder turned each time the gun was fired, moving a new bullet into position. This allowed a number of shots to be fired in a row. The revolver was popular in the mid-1800s. Colt invented a number of variations, including the Single Action Army Revolver, known as the Peacemaker.

REVOLVING CYLINDER
holds bullets in six separate chambers.

SHORT BARREL
makes the weapon easier to carry and use.

TIMELINE

1862

GATLING GUN

U.S. inventor Richard Gatling invents an early machine gun. The Gatling gun has between six and 10 barrels that fire in turn as a handle is turned. It can fire up to 200 **rounds** per minute.

SPECIFICATIONS

COLT SINGLE ACTION ARMY REVOLVER

Weight: 2 pounds 5 ounces (1,048 grams)
Length: 11 inches (279 millimeters), with short barrel
Cartridge: 0.45 Colt
Rate of fire: Six rounds per minute
Average range: 300 feet (91 meters)

SPRING inside the handle is attached to the bottom of the hammer. It pulls the hammer down to fire the bullets.

POWER PEOPLE

SAMUEL COLT

Samuel Colt (1814–1862) invented the revolver in 1836. The weapon became popular when the United States went to war with Mexico in 1846. The U.S. Army ordered thousands of revolvers. Colt became one of the wealthiest businessmen in America.

1866 ►►►

WINCHESTER RIFLE

The first Winchester repeating rifle appears in the United States. It is used by both the U.S. Army and by American Indians.

1872 ►►►

COLT 45

Samuel Colt's factories develop one of the most famous revolvers, the Colt 45.

1873 ►►►

WESTERN WEAPON

Winchester releases the Model 1873 repeating rifle. They market the weapon as "the gun that won the West."

cylinder—a drum-shaped revolving chamber with two flat ends
round—a single bullet fired by a gun

MODERN ARTILLERY

Despite improvements in artillery in the 1800s, cannons were heavy and difficult to use. They jerked back when fired, and had to be repositioned before being used again.

In 1897 the French company Schneider produced a new kind of 75 mm-**caliber** gun. It was loaded from the back and had a rifled barrel. The gun also had a liquid-filled **recoil** system. The system returned the barrel to its original position after firing. This meant that the gun could fire six times a minute, far quicker than any other big gun of the time. The gun became known simply as the "75." It was widely used in World War I (1914–1918) and inspired the design for later field guns.

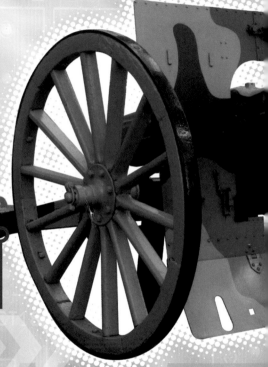

TRAIL kept gun in position during firing.

TIMELINE

1877
DUEL ACTION REVOLVER
The first double-action revolver is introduced. A single pull on the trigger pulls back the hammer and then fires the gun.

1884
MAXIM GUN
U.S. inventor Hiram Maxim develops the first fully automatic machine gun.

SPECIFICATIONS

75 MM FIELD GUN

Weight: 3,404 pounds
(1,544 kilograms)
Length: 8 feet 10 inches
(2.69 meters) barrel length
Crew: 6
Rate of fire: Around four rounds
a minute in continuous firing
Range: 7,400 yards
(6,800 meters)

INSIDE OUT

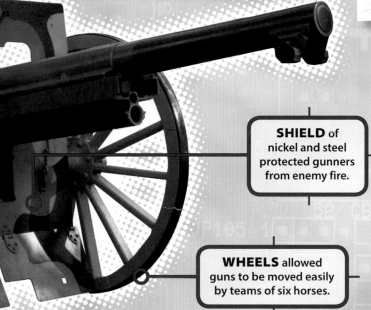

SHIELD of nickel and steel protected gunners from enemy fire.

WHEELS allowed guns to be moved easily by teams of six horses.

75 MM IN ACTION

The recoil mechanism of the 75 mm kept the gun still as it fired. That meant the crew did not have to aim the gun again after firing a shot. This made the gun quicker to fire. The French had 4,000 75-mm guns at the start of World War I and made 12,000 more during the conflict. The gun could be mounted on a truck and used to shoot down aircraft. It fired explosive shells as well as shells that released poisonous gas.

1892

AUTOMATIC HANDGUNS

Joseph Laumann invents the first automatic pistol. This self-loading gun fires repeatedly, once each time the trigger is pressed.

1897

FRENCH 75 MM

The French Army introduces the Canon de 75 modèle 1897 field gun. It is the first modern artillery weapon.

artillery—large-caliber weapons that are used on land
caliber—the diameter of ammunition used in a gun or other weapon
recoil—the kick-back of a gun after firing

MACHINE GUNS

The first machine gun had been used in the U.S. Civil War. Then, in 1884, a new kind of automatic weapon was developed.

The first fully automatic machine gun was invented in 1884 by U.S. inventor Hiram Maxim. His gun used the gas caused by firing a bullet and the energy of the recoil of the gun to move the next bullet into position. The Maxim gun could fire more than 500 bullets per minute. It used water cooling to prevent its barrel from overheating. However, this made the gun very heavy, and other inventors soon developed lighter versions, such as the Lewis gun in 1912. These new weapons led to a large number of deaths and injuries in World War I because of their rapid rates of fire.

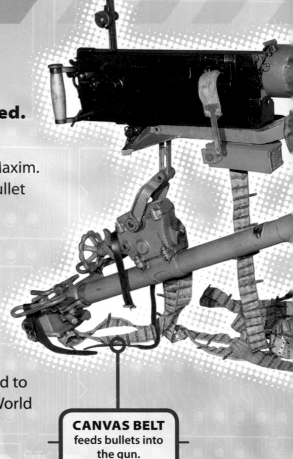

CANVAS BELT feeds bullets into the gun.

TIMELINE

1914

BIG BERTHA

The Germans develop a **howitzer** nicknamed Big Bertha. The gun fires heavy 16.5-inch (420-mm) caliber shells in a high arc. The Germans use the weapons to destroy enemy defenses.

METAL JACKET contains water to cool the gun barrel.

FOLDING LEGS provide a stable base for firing.

SPECIFICATIONS

MAXIM MACHINE GUN
Weight: 60 pounds (27.2 kilograms)
Length: 42.5 inches (107.9 centimeters)
Crew: 4
Rate of fire: 550 rounds a minute
Range: 2,187 yards (2,000 meters)

EYEWITNESS

"The enemy machine guns opened up with a murderous fire, both from the front and from some buildings which had been out of sight behind some trees. Men began to stumble and fall, then to go down like corn before a **scythe**. The cap from the head of the lad in front of me flew from his head and he fell. I stumbled over him. Even to this day I feel no shame when I say that I stayed where I was."

British Lewis gunner, Northumberland Fusiliers, Battle of Loos, 1915.

1915 ⟫⟫⟫
INTERRUPTOR GEAR
German inventors come up with an interruptor device. It allows a machine gun to fire through spinning aircraft propellors.

1916 ⟫⟫⟫
THE SOMME
German machine guns and other weapons kill about 20,000 British soldiers on the first day of the Battle of the Somme in France during World War I.

1926 ⟫⟫⟫
GODDARD'S ROCKET
U.S. inventor Robert Goddard launches the first successful liquid-fuel rocket.

howitzer—a short-barreled cannon that fires shells in a high arc
scythe—a sharp curved blade used to cut crops such as corn

FLYING BOMBS

Early in World War II (1939–1945) German scientists invented the first guided missiles. These flying bombs were called "Vengeance Weapons," or V-weapons.

The V-1 was first fired by the Germans against London in 1944. The missile could be aimed at targets up to 155 miles (250 km) away. After it took off, the rocket followed a planned course until its engine cut out at a prearranged time. Gravity then pulled the bomb down to drop on the target. The V-2 was launched in September 1944. This bomb was a rocket that could fly four times the speed of sound, or 767 miles (1,235 km) per hour. It could fly nearly straight up to the edge of the Earth's **atmosphere**. Unlike the V-1, the V-2 flew too fast to be shot down. The Germans launched more than 3,000 V-2s against **Allied** targets in the last year of the war.

WARHEAD was detonated by an igniter at the very front of the missile.

FUEL TANKS held liquid oxygen and a mixture of alcohol and water.

TIMELINE

1936
M1 GARAND
The U.S. Army introduces the M1 Garand semi-automatic rifle. It becomes the standard U.S. service rifle in World War II.

1939
KATYUSHA
Soviet forces begin to use the Katyusha. The multiple rocket launcher can destroy large areas and then speed to safety.

SPECIFICATIONS

V-2 ROCKET
Weight: 27,600 pounds
(12,500 kilograms)
Length: 45 feet 11 inches
(14 meters)
Warhead: 2,200-pound
(1,000-kilogram) bomb
Range: 200 miles (320 kilometers)
Top speed: 3,580 miles
(5,760 kilometers) per hour

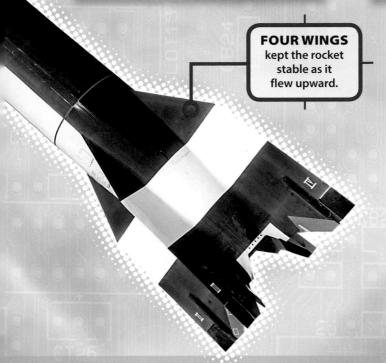

FOUR WINGS kept the rocket stable as it flew upward.

> " I heard a plane in the distance, then gunfire, and then the sound of the plane as if diving. There was an orange flash, followed by a terrific explosion. There were no sounds of bombs falling, as there were in the Blitz [the German bomb attacks on London in 1940], only the sound of the plane zooming. "

Harold Dowe describes the first V-1 attack on London in June 1944.

1942 ▶▶▶

BAZOOKA
U.S. troops begin using bazookas. These tubelike weapons fire rockets to destroy enemy tanks.

1944 ▶▶▶

V-2 ROCKET
The Germans begin using long-range V-2 rockets against targets in Britain and Belgium.

atmosphere—the layer of gas that surrounds Earth
Allied—a group of countries including the United States, England, and France that fought together in World War II
warhead—the part of a missile or rocket that explodes

ASSAULT RIFLES

In World War II, the Germans created a new type of gun called the assault rifle. It was shorter than a rifle, so it was easier to carry. It did not have a rifle's range, but it was just as accurate at short ranges.

The first assault rifle was the German Sturmgewehr 44. On its automatic setting, it continuously fired bullets from a **magazine** as long as the soldier held the trigger. Other armies also developed assault rifles. The most popular was the Russian AK-47. The AK-47 was cheap to make and easy to use. It was also highly reliable, meaning it did not malfunction or jam. It became the most widely produced of all assault rifles. Between 1949 and 1959, about 75 million AK-47s were manufactured.

REAR SIGHT enables the soldier to set the range of the target.

CURVED MAGAZINE is strong to avoid damage. It holds 30 bullets.

TIMELINE

1944
PAK 40
The Germans use the PAK 43 anti-tank gun to slow down a Soviet advance toward Germany.

1947
BALLISTIC MISSILE
The United States fires its first **ballistic** missile, the MGM-5 Corporal. It is designed to carry nuclear warheads.

SPECIFICATIONS

AK-47
Weight: 7.7 pounds
  (3.47 kilograms)
Length: 35 inches (88 centimeters)
Rate of fire: 100 rounds
  per minute (in bursts)
Maximum range: 380 yards
  (350 meters)
Cartridge: 7.62 x 39 mm

POWER PEOPLE

SOVIET GUNMAKER
Mikhail Kalashnikov
(1919–2013) was a Soviet
soldier. He used his
engineering skills to invent
the AK-47 assault rifle.
Later, he developed new
versions of the AK-47,
as well as a machine gun
called the PK. Kalashnikov
designed the weapons to
have simple, replaceable
parts. The AK-47 and PK
are still in use.

WOODEN STOCK
was later replaced by
a metal folding handle
for easier use.

1947

KALASHNIKOV
Soviet army soldier
Mikhail Kalashnikov
invents the AK-47
assault rifle.

1954

UZI
Israeli special forces begin
to use the Uzi submachine
gun, designed by Major
Uziel Gal. It includes
the magazine in the
weapon's handle.

magazine—a detachable container holding bullets for an automatic weapon
ballistic—pulled down onto a target by the force of gravity

COLD WAR MISSILES

During the Cold War (1947–1991), the United States and the Soviet Union began an arms race. Each tried to built more powerful missiles in greater numbers than the other.

These weapons were intercontinental ballistic missiles (ICBMs). Ballistic missiles burned fuel as they flew in a high arc that took them to the edge of space. Like the V-1 and V-2 flying bombs of World War II, ICBMs were pulled down onto their targets by the force of gravity. Some ICBMs carried ordinary explosives, but others were armed with **nuclear** warheads. In the 1970s the United States and the Soviet Union held a series of talks. They agreed to major reductions in the number of ICBMs they possessed.

WARHEAD
carries explosives or nuclear weapons.

ROCKET
built in stages that fell away as the fuel each stage carried was used up.

TIMELINE

1957

R-7 BALLISTIC MISSILE
The Soviet Union tests the world's first intercontinental ballistic missile, the R-7 Semyorka.

1962

CUBAN MISSILE CRISIS
The United States forces the Soviet Union to destroy secret missile bases it has built in Cuba.

SPECIFICATIONS

MINUTEMAN III ICBM

Weight: 78,000 pounds
(35,300 kilograms)
Length: 59 feet 9.5 inches
(18.2 meters)
Warhead: Nuclear
Top speed: Approx 17,507 miles
(28,176 kilometers) per hour
Range: Approx 8,000 miles
(13,000 kilometers)

IN ACTION

UNDERGROUND

The first ICBMs used liquid oxygen as fuel. The fuel could blow up by accident. The development of solid rocket fuel made the missiles safer to handle. Missiles could now be stored in silos. These were vertical tubes dug into the ground. The command centers for the missiles were also buried underground.

TRANSPORTER
allows the ICBM to be moved around and fired from anywhere in the world.

1964

M-16 RIFLE
The U.S. Army adopts the M-16 Rifle. It is widely used in jungle fighting in the Vietnam War (1955–1975).

1970

MINUTEMAN III
The United States introduces the LGM-30 Minuteman III. It is the first ICBM to carry more than one warhead.

nuclear—powered by energy released from atoms

TRIDENT

In the 1970s the United States and Soviet Union agreed to cut their supplies of ICBMs. However, they carried on building new missiles. These missiles had many warheads. They could be fired from submarines.

The Trident missile, introduced by the United States and its allies in 1979, had five separate warheads. The missile could be fired from underwater by a submarine. It flew to the edge of space, where it released its warheads. The warheads then fell back to Earth to strike different targets. Military planners believed that releasing many warheads and dummy warheads would swamp an enemy's **radar** network. That would increase the chances of more warheads reaching their targets. Trident has never been used in a war.

AEROSPIKE
reduces drag as the missile flies through the air.

SECOND STAGE
rocket motor boosts the missile into space.

TIMELINE

1972
CHAIN GUN
The first chain guns appear. They use a power source to feed bullets into the gun, which increases the rate of continuous fire.

1979
TRIDENT
The United States introduces the Trident missile. It is fired from a submerged submarine.

SPECIFICATIONS

TRIDENT MISSILE

Weight: 130,000 pounds (58,500 kilograms)

Length: 44 feet (13.41 meters)

Maximum range: More than 4,600 miles (7,360 kilometers)

Warhead: Nuclear Multiple Independently Targetable Re-entry Vehicles (MITRVs)

Propulsion: Three-stage solid-fuel rocket

INSIDE OUT

TRIDENT

Trident missiles are designed to be fired from submerged submarines. These submarines are nuclear-powered vessels. They can stay submerged at sea for months at a time. That helps protect them from enemy attack. Countries such as the United States and Great Britain have one or two submarines at sea at all times. That gives them a permanent ability to strike at an enemy when needed.

FIRST STAGE rocket motor launches the missile.

1979

M198 HOWITZER

The U.S. Army begins to use the M198 Howitzer. The weapon is towed into position, and can fire a wide range of shells.

1982

EXOCET

In the Falklands War (1982) between Britain and Argentina, British ships come under attack from Exocet missiles fired by Argentine forces.

radar—a location device that works by sending out radio signals and detecting if they are reflected back off objects

AIR-TO-AIR MISSILES

Air power is at the heart of modern warfare. Jet aircraft carry "smart" bombs that are guided to their targets by lasers or computers. Jets also carry missiles to shoot down enemy aircraft.

These air-to-air missiles work by detecting heat from the engines of aircraft. They carry **sensors** that detect **infrared** heat energy. Once the missiles are fired, the sensors guide them to follow the source of the heat. A mirror at the front of the missile reflects heat into the sensors, that work out the direction the heat is coming from. Missiles such as the AIM-9L, or Sidewinder, are designed to fly into an enemy aircraft's engines. They can also be used to destroy other missiles in mid-air.

ROTATING MIRROR reflects heat to the infrared sensor.

TIMELINE

1982
AIM-9L
British Harrier jets use Sidewinder air-to-air missiles to destroy 20 Argentine aircraft during the war over the Falkland Islands.

1982
GLOCK HANDGUN
The Austrian company Glock produces the Glock 17. The semiautomatic pistol becomes one of the most popular weapons in the world.

ches

2 miles

iles
per hour
el rocket

INFRARED ENERGY

Sidewinders and other missiles carry infrared detectors. A mirror in the front of the missile senses heat from the engines of an enemy airplane or missile. It reflects the heat to the infrared detector. The detector figures out where the heat is coming from. Then it steers the missile to keep it pointing at its target.

WARHEAD
weighs 25 pounds (11 kilograms). It is esigned to break up into many pieces.

FINS
keep the missile stable in the air, and prevent it from spinning.

DS AND PATRIOTS

he Gulf War 990–1991), Iraqis fire cud missiles at U.S.-led forces. The U.S. responds by attacking the Iraqis with Patriot missiles.

such as heat that cannot be seen by the human eye

ects energy such as light or heat

MLRS

As missiles have become more powerful, so have defenses against them. In the Gulf War the U.S.-led forces used Patriot missiles to shoot down Iraqi Scud missiles.

The Iraqis tried to locate and destroy U.S. missile launch sites. To avoid this, U.S. forces fired their missiles from mobile launchers. They also fired more than one missile at a time, in order to overwhelm enemy defenses. The Multiple Launch Rocket System (MLRS) is a mobile launcher attached to a truck. It can be used anywhere. After it has fired, the launcher moves. This stops the enemy from locating it. The modern MLRS is based on the Katyusha weapon developed by the Soviet Union in World War II.

TIMELINE

1991 >>>

THE GULF WAR
U.S. forces fire the largest-ever nighttime MLRS attack against Iraqi positions.

1997 >>>

JDAM
U.S. forces introduce the Joint Direct Attack Munition, or JDAM. It converts ordinary bombs into "smart" weapons that can detect targets.

SPECIFICAT

AIM-9L SIDEWI
Weight: 188 pound
(85.3 kilograms)
Length: 9 feet 11 in
(3.02 meters)
Maximum range: 2
(35.4 kilometers)
Top speed: 1,919 m
(3,087 kilometers)
Propulsion: Solid-fu

de

1986 ⟫⟫
PEACEKEEPER ICBM
The United States
introduces the LGM-118
ICBM, nicknamed
the Peacekeeper.

199
SCU
In t
(1
S

infrared—a type of energy
sensors—a device that det

PISTONS raise the missile firing position. They can rotate to face in any direction.

M270 (1980–2003)
Weight: 55,000 pounds
(24,950 kilograms)
Length: 22 feet 6 inches (6.85 meters)
Crew: 3
Rate of fire: 12 rockets in under
1 minute
Top speed: 40 miles (64 kilometers)
per hour

IN ACTION

TWO PODS
hold six rockets or
missiles. They can
all be fired within
60 seconds.

THE GULF WAR

In 1990 Iraqi leader Saddam Hussein sent his troops to occupy Kuwait. U.S.-led forces who arrived to help Kuwait used numerous MLRS weapons. They fired missiles at Iraqi positions until Iraqi forces were driven out of Kuwait. The U.S.-led forces used MLRS missiles to attack the **armored** vehicles of the retreating Iraqi army.

BARS protect the driver's
window from any debris that
might break the glass.

2000 ▶▶▶

TAC-50
The McMillan Tac-50 Sniper Rifle goes into service. It has a firing range of over 1 mile (1.6 km).

2012 ▶▶▶

M777 HOWITZER
A U.S. M777 Howitzer in Afghanistan accurately shells rebels at a range of 22 miles (36 km).

armored—protected by sheets of metal or steel

NEW GENERATION

Late in the 1900s, U.S. armed forces came up with a new kind of infantry weapon. This was a light machine gun, or squad automatic weapon (SAW).

Most earlier machine guns were heavy weapons. They required two men to operate them. The light machine gun was designed to be carried and used by an individual soldier. It had greater firepower than **infantry** rifles. It used belt-fed ammunition like a machine gun, which gave it a high firing rate. The M249 has a short stock, or handle. This makes it easier to carry during a parachute jump. The weapon is also easier to handle in cramped spaces, such as during street fighting.

AIR-COOLED barrel can be easily replaced if it jams.

FOLDING LEGS support barrel during firing, increasing accuracy.

INTO THE FUTURE

FN F2000
The F2000 is a Belgian assault rifle. It uses a "bullpup" design in which the trigger is positioned in front of the gun's magazine. This allows the weapon to be shorter than earlier guns, but without any loss of fire power or accuracy.

BOX CASING beneath the weapon holds the linked belt of cartridges.

SPECIFICATIONS

M249
Weight: 22 pounds (10 kilograms), loaded
Length: 40.75 inches (1.03 meters)
Rate of fire: 100 rounds per minute, sustained firing
Maximum range: 2.23 miles (3.6 kilometers)
Cartridge: 5.56 x 45 mm NATO

WAR ON TERROR

The light machine gun has been one of the most common weapons in recent wars. U.S. forces have faced terrorists, called insurgents, in Afghanistan and Iraq. The weapons are light enough to be carried by soldiers on foot patrol. If the soldiers come under attack, they can defend themselves at long range.

TOMAHAWK MISSILE

The Tomahawk missile has been in service since the 1990s. Its most recent model carries a camera. Photographs allow an operator watching remotely to retarget the missile as it flies.

infantry—soldiers who fight on foot

GLOSSARY

Allied (AL-lyd)—related to a group of countries including the United States, England, and France that fought together in World War II

armored (AR-muhrd)—protected by sheets of metal or steel

artillery (ar-TIL-uh-ree)—large-caliber weapons that are used on land

atmosphere (AT-mos-fear)—the layer of gas that surrounds the Earth

ballistic (bu-LIS-tic)—moved by the force of gravity

bayonet (bay-uh-NET—a long, sharp blade attached to the front of a rifle for stabbing

caliber (KA-luh-buhr)—the diameter of ammunition used in a gun or other weapon

cylinder (SI-luhn-duhr)—a drum-shaped revolving chamber with two flat ends

howitzer (HOU-uht-sur)—a short-barreled cannon that fires shells in a high arc

infantry (IN-fuhn-tree)—soldiers who fight on foot

infrared (in-fruh-RED)—a type of energy such as heat that cannot be seen by the human eye

magazine (MAG-uh-zeen)—a detachable container holding bullets for an automatic weapon

missile (MISS-uhl)—an object that is thrown or fired toward a target

nuclear (NOO-clee-ur)—powered by energy released from atoms

recoil (RI-koil)—the kick-back of a gun after firing

rifled (RYE-fuld)—with a spiral groove carved inside the barrel

radar (RAY-dar)—a location device that works by sending out radio signals and detecting if they are reflected back off objects

round (ROWND)—a single bullet fired by a gun

scythe (SITHE)—a sharp curved blade used to cut crops such as corn

sensor (SEN-sur)—a device that detects energy such as light or heat

smoothbore (SMOOTHE-bor)—having no rifling inside the barrel

volley (VOL-ee)—a number of bullets or other missiles all fired at the same time

warhead (WAR-hed)—the part of a missile or rocket that explodes

READ MORE

Lanser, Amanda. *World War II by the Numbers.* America at War by the Numbers. North Mankato, Minn.: Capstone Press, 2016

Ripley, Tim. *Torpedoes, Missiles, and Cannons: Physics Goes to War.* STEM on the Battlefield. Minneapolis: Lerner Publications, 2018

Rowell, Rebecca. *Building Rockets.* Engineering Challenges. Mendota Heights, Minn.: North Star Editions, 2017

INTERNET SITES

Use FactHound to find Internet sites related to this book.

Visit www.facthound.com

Just type in 9781515791973 and go.

 Super-cool stuff! Check out projects, games and lots more at
www.capstonekids.com

INDEX